Rebecca Currington &
Patricia Mitchell

EVERYDAY

Comfort

Spiritual Refreshment
for Women

BARBOUR
PUBLISHING

© 2008 by Barbour Publishing, Inc.

ISBN 978-1-60260-211-3

All rights reserved. No part of this publication may be reproduced or transmitted for commercial purposes, except for brief quotations or printed reviews, without written permission of the publisher.

Churches and other noncommercial interests may reproduce portions of this book without the express written permission of Barbour Publishing, provided that the text does not exceed 500 words and that the text is not material quoted from another publisher. When reproducing text from this book, include the following credit line: "From *Spiritual Refreshment for Women: Everyday Comfort*, published by Barbour Publishing, Inc. Used by permission."

Unless otherwise marked, scripture quotations are taken from the *Holy Bible: New International Version*®. NIV®. (North American Edition)®. Copyright 1973, 1978, 1984 by International Bible Society. Used by permission of Zondervan. All rights reserved.

Scripture quotations marked NKJV are taken from the *New King James Version*®. Copyright © 1982 by Thomas Nelson, Inc. Used by permission. All rights reserved.

Scripture quotations marked AMP are taken from the *Amplified*® *Bible,* Copyright © 1954, 1958, 1962, 1964, 1965, 1987 by The Lockman Foundation. Used by permission. (www.Lockman.org)

Scripture quotations marked NCV are taken from the *New Century Version*®. Copyright © 2005 by Thomas Nelson, Inc. Used by permission. All rights reserved.

Scripture quotations marked MSG are taken from THE MESSAGE, copyright © by Eugene H.Peterson 1993, 1994, 1995, 1996, 2000, 2001, 2002. Used by permission of NavPress Publishing Group.

Scripture quotations marked KJV are taken from the King James Version of the Bible.

Scripture quotations marked NLT are taken from *The Holy Bible, New Living Translation.* Copyright © 1996, 2004. Used by permission of Tyndale House Publishers, Incorporated, Wheaton, Illinois 60189. All rights reserved.

Scripture quotations marked NASB are taken from the *New American Standard Bible*®. Copyright © 1960, 1962, 1963, 1968, 1971, 1972, 1973, 1975, 1977, 1995 by The Lockman Foundation. Used by permission.

Cover design: Kirk DouPonce, DogEared Design

Writing and compilation by Rebecca Currington and Patricia Mitchell in association with Snapdragon Group℠.

Published by Barbour Publishing, Inc., P.O. Box 719, Uhrichsville, Ohio 44683, www.barbourbooks.com.

Our mission is to publish and distribute inspirational products offering exceptional value and biblical encouragement to the masses.

Member of the
Evangelical Christian
Publishers Association

Printed in India.

Contents

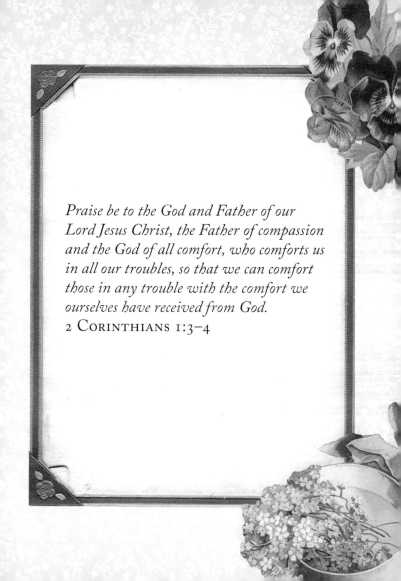

Praise be to the God and Father of our Lord Jesus Christ, the Father of compassion and the God of all comfort, who comforts us in all our troubles, so that we can comfort those in any trouble with the comfort we ourselves have received from God.

2 CORINTHIANS 1:3–4

Introduction

This world is a dangerous place. No one comes through it untouched—not the dearest saint or the meanest sinner. But for those who put their trust in God, this world is just a temporary home. One day we will reside in heaven where love, joy, and peace prevail. Until then, He has promised us His comfort. No matter what we face in this lifetime, no matter what calamity comes our way—great or small—God has vowed never to let go of our hands.

Everyday Comfort was created to remind you that you are never alone in your troubles. If you trust Him, He will be there in the good times and the bad, pouring out His love, providing wisdom and guidance, listening to your hurting heart, shouldering your burdens, and bringing you safely through to the other side.

As you read, we pray that you will feel God's warm and sustaining comfort in your life.

Adversity

"Do not fear or be dismayed;
tomorrow go out against them,
for the LORD is with you."

2 CHRONICLES 20:17 NKJV

Adversity, calamity, hardship, misfortune, trouble, hard times—no matter what you call them, these painful episodes are part and parcel of the human experience. But you can choose to not let them bring you down, fill you with fear, and steal your attention from the blessings God has placed in your life. Look adversity square in the eye and know that your God—the God of all comfort—has an answer.

A friend loves at all times,
and a brother is born for adversity.

PROVERBS 17:17 NKJV

When you give your heart and life to God, the Bible says Jesus Christ becomes your friend and your brother—and that changes everything. You aren't alone when adversity strikes. You've become a member of God's family and part of His circle of friends. His resources are marshaled in your defense, and His loving Holy Spirit—the Bible calls Him the Comforter—is with you constantly.

Affliction

The righteous person faces
many troubles, but the Lord
comes to the rescue each time.

Psalm 34:19 nlt

An affliction is any source of constant suffering in your life. That might be poverty or sickness or anxiety—only you know what you are facing. You may think that no one understands. But God does. No matter where you are, He's right there with you. Trust Him, and He will show you the way out, the way around, or the way through, and He will never leave your side.

Our light affliction, which is
but for a moment, worketh for us
a far more exceeding and
eternal weight of glory.

2 CORINTHIANS 4:17 KJV

Have you ever wondered why God doesn't
just put an end to your troubles and give you
a free pass from pain and suffering? After
all, He can do anything! God doesn't bring
suffering to your life, but sometimes He will
ask you to walk through it for reasons known
only to Him. But you can be sure of this
God will use your affliction to make you
stronger and more secure in your faith.

Agreement

All of you should be in agreement,
understanding each other, loving each
other as family, being kind and humble.

1 PETER 3:8 NCV

God knows that much of our strength and comfort comes from other people—our friends and loved ones. But what if there is no one in your life who can encourage and lift you, no one who can understand what you are going through, no one who can pray with you? Don't lose heart. Set yourself in agreement with God and His will for your life. As you agree with God, He will send others to agree with you.

This is the confidence
(the assurance, the privilege of
boldness) which we have in Him:
[we are sure] that if we ask anything
(make any request) according to
His will (in agreement with His own
plan), He listens to and hears us.

1 JOHN 5:14 AMP

What could be better than to be in full agreement with the One who knows the beginning from the end, someone who understands all the options and sees all the solutions? Take comfort in the fact that your prayer partner, your friend, and your comrade is God Himself. You can take any request to Him with the assurance that He will hear you. As you do, be sure to thank Him for His help.

Anxiety

Cast all your anxiety on him
because he cares for you.
1 Peter 5:7

This world gives us plenty of reasons to worry. Danger looms around every corner even for the wise and well-informed. People try all kinds of things to escape worry and anxiety—recreation, yoga, video games, sleep, to name just a few. But in the end there is only one sure remedy. God says to cast all your anxiety on Him. He's big enough to handle anything that comes your way.

Do not be anxious about anything, but in everything, by prayer and petition, with thanksgiving, present your requests to God. And the peace of God, which transcends all understanding, will guard your hearts and your minds in Christ Jesus.

PHILIPPIANS 4:6–7

What does it mean to "cast your care on God"? Start by opening your heart and telling Him about your fears, your worries, those things that make you feel anxious. Once you've done that, thank Him for taking all that worry off your hands. As you give up your anxious thoughts to Him, He gives you something back—His perfect peace.

Aspirations

I do not mean that I am already as
God wants me to be. I have not yet
reached that goal, but I continue
trying to reach it and to make it mine.

PHILIPPIANS 3:12 NCV

Are you driven by that little voice inside
you that keeps telling you to reach higher, try
harder, and never give up until you attain a
certain goal in your life? If your goal is within
the scope of God's will, that voice is almost
certainly His. It isn't His will for you to seek
out temporal things like money, fame, or
possessions. But He does want you to aspire to
become everything He has created you to be.

> What matters most to me
> is to finish what God started.
>
> ACTS 20:24 MSG

Who God wants you to be includes what He wants you to do. He has a specific plan for every single person in this world—including you. You may not have a grand talent or an extraordinary intellect, but you have been given everything you need to carry out your mission in life—your calling. Pray each day that God will help you find and complete the work He has given you to do.

Assurance

Faith is the assurance
of things hoped for.

HEBREWS 11:1 NASB

We human beings have plenty of insecurities, so you shouldn't be ashamed to admit you have a few. The good news is that you don't have to let them shape your life. When you place your faith in God, they will be replaced by the steadfast assurance that those things you hope for are yours through His love and grace. No more wondering if you're good enough or lovable enough or smart enough. In God's eyes you are perfect.

My flesh and my heart may fail,
but God is the strength of my heart
and my portion forever.

PSALM 73:26

God has everything under control. That's not just a pie-in-the-sky concept—it's a fact. God knows and understands you from the inside out. And when you place your life in His hands, you can be certain that in the good times and the bad times, the happy times and the heartbreaking times, you will always have someone to depend on, someone to fall back on, someone stronger than any challenge you could possibly face.

Battles

O Sovereign LORD,
my strong deliverer, who shields
my head in the day of battle...

PSALM 140:7

You may be facing a battle right now—a fight for your health, your children, your finances, for example. As the battle rages, know that you are not facing the enemy alone. Your God is fighting by your side. He is leading the charge to bring you safely through. Put your confidence in Him. Follow His lead, and let His unmatched strength be a comfort to you.

It is God who arms me
with strength and makes my way
perfect. He makes my feet like the
feet of a deer; he enables me to
stand on the heights. He trains my
hands for battle; my arms can
bend a bow of bronze.

PSALM 18:32–34

It could be that you have been battling for
so long that you are feeling weak, exhausted,
and ready to throw in the towel. Close your
eyes and rest your troubled mind. Don't
worry; even when you're resting, God and
His army are still fighting on your behalf.
And they won't stop until the battle is won.
It's all right to take a break and let Him
carry you for a while.

Beauty

Don't be concerned about the outward
beauty of fancy hairstyles, expensive
jewelry, or beautiful clothes. You should
clothe yourselves instead with the beauty
that comes from within, the unfading
beauty of a gentle and quiet spirit,
which is so precious to God.

1 Peter 3:3–4 NLT

Twenty-first-century women are exposed to an almost impossible standard of beauty. And the message is unrelenting. In such an environment, every little flaw or blemish can be devastating. God says that outward beauty is of no consequence unless there is beauty on the inside. After all, even the most beautiful woman cannot hope to keep her looks for long. The beautiful, godly soul, however, lives forever.

> "The LORD does not look at the things man looks at. Man looks at the outward appearance, but the LORD looks at the heart."
>
> 1 SAMUEL 16:7

Who says what is beautiful and what is not? It would seem that the creator of a work of art would be the one whose opinion matters most. For the creator, every nuance, every brushstroke, every indention in the clay has meaning. God created you—with intention and purpose. You are His work of art. In His eyes, you are beautiful in every way, inside and out.

Belief

Once made perfect, [Jesus] became the source of eternal salvation for all who obey him.

HEBREWS 5:9

The older we are the more we understand the futility of this life. But there is great comfort in knowing that this life is not the end. Through His Son, Jesus Christ, God has provided a remedy for sin, with its constant menu of corruption and death. No longer are we headed only for the grave—but to the grave and beyond. This sacred belief is our blessed hope.

Jesus said to her, "I am the resurrection and the life. He who believes in me will live, even though he dies; and whoever lives and believes in me will never die. Do you believe this?"

JOHN 11:25–26

Your beliefs say a lot about your future. For example, believing that hard work leads to success will help you meet your goals. Believing that true love lasts forever will help you remain steadfast in your marriage. And believing that God has promised you life everlasting will allow you to continue to value yourself even as your body ages and your earthly life winds down. Beliefs are important, and those invested in God pay the biggest dividends of all.

Belonging

You are all the same in Christ
Jesus. You belong to Christ.

GALATIANS 3:28–29 NCV

We all want to belong. It's a normal human instinct. Unfortunately, our culture places value on so many things that have no lasting meaning—where we live, how we dress, where our children go to school. Comfort yourself with the truth that God values you for who you really are deep inside, nothing more, nothing less. You are His magnificent creation and a member of His royal family.

You belong to Him.

Whether we live or die,
we belong to the Lord.

ROMANS 14:8

Have you ever been abandoned by a friend or family member? There are few feelings worse than a lost relationship. That's why it's so important to know that once you belong to the Lord, you will always belong to Him. Even when you mess up and make poor choices, your heavenly Father will not abandon you. For the remainder of this life and the life to come—you are His!

Bereavement

[Jesus said,] "Blessed are those who mourn, for they will be comforted."

MATTHEW 5:4

Dear Sharleen & family,

Losing someone you love is one of the most devastating experiences in life—whether it be a friend or relative, your child or your spouse, even a beloved pet who has brightened your life and helped ward off loneliness. God understands your grief. He gave up His own precious Son for you. He knows the anguish of losing someone who meant everything to Him. Let Him comfort you as only He can.

May His words give you peace & strength.

Love & prayers, Paul & Elly

He will swallow up death forever.
The Sovereign LORD will wipe
away the tears from all faces.

ISAIAH 25:8

When you lose someone you love, you
might wonder what possible comfort anyone could give you—even God. But there
is comfort in looking beyond the grave,
beyond this life, and knowing that your
separation from that beloved one, while
excruciating, is not permanent. The two of
you will meet again in a place where death
no longer has meaning. Even in the darkest
moments, God lights your way with hope.

Betrayal

He will shelter you with his wings. His faithful promises are your armor and protection.

PSALM 91:4 NLT

Betrayal is such a bitter word. It's always personal. You invested yourself in someone and that person purposefully turned away. Whenever you place your trust in a human being, you risk betrayal. We just don't have the wherewithal to remain 100 percent faithful. But God does. And He promises never to betray the trust you place in Him. He'll even be there to pick up the pieces, to comfort you, when others fail you.

"I'll marry you for good—forever!
I'll marry you true and proper,
in love and tenderness.
Yes, I'll marry you and neither leave
you nor let you go. You'll know me,
God, for who I really am."

HOSEA 2:19–20 MSG

No other betrayal is quite as painful as the loss of marital love and fidelity. All those bright promises of happily ever after lie broken in the dust. If you're feeling this closest of all betrayals, God wants to comfort you with His proposal. He wants to serve as your spiritual husband, providing you with the love, faithfulness, compassion, guidance, understanding, and caring you so desperately need. He won't fail you.

Boldness

[Jesus has] been through weakness and testing, experienced it all—all but the sin. So let's walk right up to him and get what he is so ready to give. Take the mercy, accept the help.

HEBREWS 4:15–16 MSG

God is big and powerful and holy. Even the most impressive woman pales in His shadow. Good sense would dictate that we keep our distance, interacting only when we are out of options. But in this case, good sense takes a backseat to God's ways. He has invited us to be bold with our requests, comfortable in His presence. He has called us His children. What a wonderful privilege!

> In Christ we can come before
> God with freedom and without fear.
> We can do this through faith in Christ.
>
> EPHESIANS 3:12 NCV

Our boldness before God resides in His
authority, not in our own. He has set the
stage for our adoption as His children,
heirs to blessing and eternal life. Our part
is simply to accept, to say "yes" and take our
places around His table. Through faith in
His love and grace, we gain bold access to
His presence. Once you place your faith in
who He is, you will know who you are.

Broken Heart

The LORD is close to the
brokenhearted and saves those who
are crushed in spirit.

PSALM 34:18

God's love is manifest at all times in our
lives, but never so much as when our hearts
are breaking. It is then that we experience
His compassion and comfort in ways we
cannot even imagine during the good times.
When you've suffered a betrayal or loss or
disappointment, when life threatens to bury
you under the cold, hard ground, God is
there with hope and comfort in your darkest
hour.

> [God] heals the brokenhearted
> and binds up their wounds.
>
> PSALM 147:3

God has promised to see you through the
most painful hours of your life, but His love
and compassion don't end there. If you let
Him, He will pick up the pieces of your broken heart and put them back together again.
Your tears are precious to your heavenly
Father, your suffering never wasted. You can
trust Him to understand your sorrow—even
enter into it with you—as He brings healing
and new life from the ashes.

Sharleen, your broken-heart
over your mom's death
is never wasted. Just
imagine Him
healing you!

Burdens

Praise be to the Lord, to God our Savior, who daily bears our burdens.

PSALM 68:19

Women are burden-carriers of the first order. In addition to our own responsibilities and troubles, we often take on those of others. God says, "You can't carry all that by yourself. Let Me help." Then He comes up alongside and helps us shoulder the load. If you feel you are faltering beneath your burdens, tell Him you are ready to let Him lend a hand. He won't touch your stuff unless you ask Him. But when you do, He'll step right up.

> "Come to me, all of you who
> are weary and carry heavy
> burdens, and I will give you rest."
>
> MATTHEW 11:28 NLT

God isn't going to snap His fingers and
make your financial woes disappear. You
will still have to deal with your problem
children and bear responsibility for your
aging parents or your boss's unrealistic
expectations. But God will faithfully provide solutions, like help from other human
hands, wisdom, and counsel. And He'll give
you a place of rest along the way—like
a well-watered oasis in the desert.

Challenges

Just as the sufferings of Christ flow
over into our lives, so also through
Christ our comfort overflows.

2 CORINTHIANS 1:5

Are you facing an extreme challenge in your life—perhaps your children are rebelling, your marriage is floundering, your health is in peril, your finances are out of control? Jesus had challenges as well—big ones. He was subjected to all manner of indignities, pain, and suffering. Although He submitted Himself to those cruel circumstances for our sake, in God's perfect time He rose up and conquered both sin and death.

Because the Sovereign LORD helps me,
I will not be disgraced. Therefore have
I set my face like flint, and I know
I will not be put to shame.

ISAIAH 50:7

Even though God uses certain negative
situations in our lives to strengthen and
equip us, He doesn't cause our adverse circumstances. Most often they are the result
of our own poor choices or the poor choices
of others. Ask God to accomplish His will in
your life and then help you rise up and con-
quer your challenges—just as Jesus did.

Children

This is what the LORD says. . .
"I will comfort you as a
mother comforts her child."

ISAIAH 66:12–13 NCV

Raising children is the most difficult, rewarding, exhausting, beautiful, chaotic, amazing job a woman can have. It's a mixed bag of dynamic emotions, pure affections, and unwavering devotion. When her children need comfort, a true mother instinctively provides it. God is the same way with His children. When you are hurting, He is there without fail, reaching out to you.

> He gives childless couples
> a family, gives them joy as
> the parents of children.
>
> PSALM 113:9 MSG

Some women live with a strong, unrelenting longing for children that seems to go unanswered. If you are dealing with this heartache, you can know that God has placed the desire to be a mother in your heart—and not just to frustrate you. Perhaps it's time to consider other possibilities. We are ourselves adopted into His family, and someone must mother those young in the faith. Ask God to help you find the children He has ordained for you.

Confidence

In the fear of the LORD
there is strong confidence.

PROVERBS 14:26 NKJV

Everywhere we look there are messages
about how to be filled with inner confidence.
Take this course, dress this way, speak your
mind, and the ever-popular suggestion to
reach down deep inside yourself. Unfortunately, those tactics only give the illusion of
confidence. True confidence comes from
knowing that almighty God, the creator and
sustainer of the universe, is backing you up
and showing you the way.

Do not throw away your confidence;
it will be richly rewarded.

HEBREWS 10:35

Circumstances of life often tend to erode
our confidence and leave us feeling weak
and unproductive. When you encounter those
times, don't throw away your confidence—
redirect it. Make sure that it is anchored in
God's character, resources, and unwavering
faithfulness. People will fail you, and you
will even fail yourself at times, but God will
never let you down.

Creativity

By him all things were created:
things in heaven and on earth, visible
and invisible, whether thrones or
powers or rulers or authorities; all
things were created by him and for him.

COLOSSIANS 1:16

God is quite the Master Artist, and He takes His work seriously. You may have noticed the delicious burnt umber of the sunset, the yellow-green waters of Lake Superior, or a towering stand of timber. Yes, that was His work. The entire universe is His gallery. But those spectacular pieces are little more than eye candy compared to His human creations. God expressed His extraordinary creativity when He created you—and He calls you His best work.

> So God created human beings
> in his own image. In the
> image of God he created them;
> male and female he created them.

GENESIS 1:27 NLT

Did you know you were created in God's image? No wonder you feel that urge to create. Don't hold back. Open your mind to new thoughts, new mental pictures, new ways of doing things. Ask God to open wide the gates of your creativity. You may not be an artist or a musician or a writer, but God has given each person—including you—a creative bent, and He is anxious for you to find yours.

Danger

"Whoever listens to me will live
in safety and be at ease,
without fear of harm."

PROVERBS 1:33

Remember the Ten Commandments?
Many people think making those rules was
God's way of asserting His authority, making
sure we all know He's in charge. But a closer
look shows that He is more interested in
keeping us safe in a dangerous world. Just as
you institute guidelines to keep your children out of harm's way, our loving heavenly
Father has done the same.

> The wise see danger ahead
> and avoid it.
>
> PROVERBS 27:12 NCV

It probably isn't possible to avoid all danger in this treacherous world, but living wisely and paying attention to God's Word can give you a real advantage. Parents often establish rules for their family that the kids don't understand. But parents know the rules are for the kids' safety and well-being. Sometimes you won't see the reason for God's rules either, but obeying them will help you skirt danger and abide in safety.

Debt

Let no debt remain outstanding,
except the continuing debt
to love one other.

ROMANS 13:8

It's rare to find anyone in our current culture who is truly debt free. Financial advisors even contend that some calculated debt is an advantage. The trouble is that debt can quickly spiral out of control. If you're facing a mountain of debt each month, you know how hopeless it feels. God wants you to be free—free to fulfill your destiny. If you ask Him, He'll help you find a plan to free yourself.

God called you to be free,
but do not use your freedom
as an excuse to do what
pleases your sinful self.

GALATIANS 5:13 NCV

Freeing yourself from debt will take some
work. It may mean sacrifices, changing your
way of doing things, replacing bad habits
with good ones. But you can be sure that
God will be behind you all the way. He'll
provide comfort, wisdom, and encouragement along the way. He'll even give you
favor with your creditors. And the day you
wake up and realize you are free will be
worth it all.

Deception

Jesus answered, "I am the way, and the
truth, and the life. The only way to
the Father is through me."

JOHN 14:6 NCV

If you've ever been deceived, you know how
devastating it can be. Not only do you feel
hurt, but your sense of trust is shaken, as
well. Maybe that's why God so often reminds
us in the Bible that He represents truth,
pure and simple. There is no deception in
Him. He won't try to secure your love with
empty promises. He can be trusted. Wrap
your heart and mind around that truth and
let it heal you.

The heart is deceitful above
all things and beyond cure.
Who can understand it?

JEREMIAH 17:9

God knows we are vulnerable to deception not only from others but also from
our own hearts. We humans have an innate
inclination to lie to ourselves. But God has
a remedy. He encourages us to follow Him,
listen to Him, trust His words. Can you
trust your heart? The sweet Holy Spirit—the
Comforter—will help you keep your heart
clean and filled with truth.

Defeat

We have troubles all around us,
but we are not defeated. We do not
know what to do, but we do not
give up the hope of living.

2 CORINTHIANS 4:8 NCV

Sometimes it seems like one little thing goes wrong, and it starts a chain reaction of disappointments and negative expectations. The power of this process is in its cumulative nature. Like the straw that breaks the camel's back, one defeat sits on another until it brings us down. God says His mercies are new every morning. Each day is a new beginning. He wants us to put our troubles behind us and cling to the hope of living.

> With God we will
> gain the victory.
>
> PSALM 108:13

God wants us to understand that even though we will experience troubles, we are immune to lasting defeat. Even when we lose, we win because God sees to it that we gain wisdom and understanding from our losses. He reaches out to us with comfort and consolation. Each loss actually brings us closer to victory. Learn from your defeats, and then turn your back on them and reach for God's mercies.

Depression

Be strong and take heart,
all you who hope in the LORD.
PSALM 31:24

For those who live with the darkness of depression, no one has to explain the pain and despair. It's not the kind of thing that can be reasoned away. It's just there, pulling them down, keeping them captive. If you suffer depression, you should know that God doesn't intend for His children to live in despair. He has an answer for you. Visit your doctor for a check-up, find someone to talk to. When you do what you can, He will be there to do the rest.

Why are you downcast, O my soul?
Why so disturbed within me? Put your
hope in God, for I will yet praise him,
my Savior and my God.

PSALM 42:5–6

Depression is often a physiological problem, but just as often it's a result of adverse
circumstances. If events in your life have
left you in the depths of despair, God wants
you to know that you are not alone. He is
right there with you. Even when others don't
understand, He does. Others only see who
you are on the outside, but He knows all
about you, inside and out. He knows how
to comfort you. Reach out to Him and
He will reach back.

Desires

May He grant you according
to your heart's desire, and fulfill
all your purpose.

PSALM 20:4 NKJV

What is it you want with all your heart—
true love, a great job, children? Only you
know what it is. You needn't hold back.
Because you are His child, God longs to give
you the things that would make you happy.
There are some conditions, though. Like
any good parent, He balances what you want
with what He knows is good for you. He isn't
interested in your temporary, superficial
happiness. He wants to give you more than
you ever imagined.

> Delight yourself in the LORD
> and he will give you the
> desires of your heart.
>
> PSALM 37:4

As you get to know God better, as you bask in His love and care, your desires will change. Selfishness and unwholesome desires will fade away. You will begin to understand and desire those things He desires for you—those things that will resonate in your heart and bring you true happiness. God created you, and He knows you better than you know yourself. Trust Him to give you the desires of your heart.

Determination

"Be strong and do not give up,
for your work will be rewarded."
2 CHRONICLES 15:7

Have you ever watched a marathon? They can be pretty boring until the runners get to the final few miles. Some are so exhausted that they can barely stay on their feet. You want to scream, "Give it up! It's just a race!" but they don't give up. The runners are determined to finish. They understand the reward that awaits them on the other side of the finish line, so they keep pushing.

That's the kind of determination it takes to please God.

Let us hold fast the confession
of our hope without wavering,
for He who promised is faithful.

HEBREWS 10:23 NKJV

God doesn't want you to ever give up on becoming the person He created you to be. He wants to see you follow the dream He's placed in your heart, develop your talent, fulfill your mission in life. Sure, sometimes you will feel like giving up, trying something easier. But remember that a reward waits for you on the other side of the finish line— a reward more wonderful than you can imagine. You can count on that because God has promised.

Discipleship

Jesus said, "If you hold to my teaching,
you are really my disciples. Then you
will know the truth, and the truth will
set you free."

JOHN 8:31–32

Sometimes trying to follow the teachings of
Jesus makes you feel as if you're going two
steps forward and one step back. The "step
back" shouldn't leave you discouraged, however. Instead, let it encourage you to turn to
God with a humble heart. He promises to
send His Holy Spirit to fill you with strength,
confidence, and perseverance as you step
forward again in His footsteps.

> [Jesus said,] "A new command I give you: Love one another. As I have loved you, so you must love one another. By this all men will know that you are my disciples, if you love one another."
>
> JOHN 13:34–35

He's hard to love." "She's not a lovable person." Whose name comes to mind? This is the very person Jesus invites you to love the same way He loves you—with a heart open to forgiveness, kindness, and compassion. As you follow in Jesus' footsteps, let the Holy Spirit replace your feelings of dislike, anger, or resentment with a disciple's willingness to reach out in genuine fellowship and Christian love.

Divorce

My comfort in my suffering is this:
Your promise preserves my life.
PSALM 119:50

Divorce can leave lifelong consequences in its wake, even affecting and infecting future relationships. Though you may be facing some of the negative results of divorce, God offers a positive message: He forgives you, regardless of what you may have said and done. And He comforts you with His unchanging promise of everlasting love and eternal life. Just ask Him, and He'll tell you as many times as you need to hear it.

Mercy triumphs over judgment!
JAMES 2:13

Divorce isn't really just a struggle between two people. It usually ends up involving friends and family. It's difficult to come away without some bitter feelings toward someone. Emotions so strong make it very tough to forgive. But that's exactly what you must do before you can move on with your life. Ask God to help you let go of any bitterness you might be harboring. Then turn your face to the future and the bright tomorrows ahead.

Doubts

What if some did not have faith?
Will their lack of faith nullify
God's faithfulness? Not at all!

ROMANS 3:3–4

When you doubt God's power and ability, you then place your trust in someone or something else. Sooner or later, you're sadly disappointed, because no one is capable of meeting your spiritual needs, and no thing or activity on earth can meet your deep longing for fulfillment. Only God can! Throw doubt aside and come back to Him. No matter how long you have been gone, He has been faithful to you and will be there for you.

[Jesus] said to them, "Why are you troubled, and why do doubts rise in your minds?"

LUKE 24:38

God never condemns you for doubting. Instead, He invites you to use doubt as a springboard to find out more about Him, His love for you, and His plan for you to live with Him in heaven. Give voice to your doubts, looking to Him for answers through Bible study, meditation, and the counsel of mature Christians. Let your doubts work to take you toward a greater appreciation of your God and His unwavering love for you.

Dreams

For God is working in you,
giving you the desire and the
power to do what pleases him.

PHILIPPIANS 2:13 NLT

When "no" evicts your cherished hopes and dreams, bitterness often moves in—and stays. Avoid the temptation to let disappointment replace your dreams, and instead let God's Spirit find a home in your heart. Tell Him your dreams then listen for His answer. Discover His "yes" in the blessings around you, in your abilities and opportunities, and in the work He has given you to do. Let following Him be your dream come true!

Who hopes for what he already has?
But if we hope for what we do not
yet have, we wait for it patiently.

ROMANS 8:24–25

God has no desire for you to be misled by lies that masquerade as truth. While popular myths and wishful thinking sometimes offer feel-good solutions, God has given you His Word so you can know the difference between dreams and reality. He invites you to immerse yourself, not in wishful thinking that evaporates in a day, but in sound teachings that will lead you to the truth and remain with you throughout eternity.

Duty

Whatever work you do, do your best.
ECCLESIASTES 9:10 NCV

By necessity, many people work in jobs they don't like or feel suited for. For them, work is a duty rather than a dream. If you find yourself in that situation, there is something you can do. Take one day at a time and focus your attention on your responsibilities for that day. Give it your all as a token of your love and respect for God. You will either begin to see your job differently, or God will find you a new assignment. He always rewards the diligent.

> Commit to the LORD
> whatever you do, and your
> plans will succeed.
>
> PROVERBS 16:3

God is never without a plan, and He has one for your life as well. There will be times when you wonder how your current job could be part of that plan. Maybe you are just spinning your wheels, doing your duty. Be assured that God has a purpose for everything you put your hand to. Perhaps it's a lesson you need to learn or a skill you will one day need. Begin to look at your job in the context of God's wisdom, and you'll see His hand in all you do.

Emotion

Weeping may remain for a night,
but rejoicing comes in the morning.

PSALM 30:5

When your emotions leave you sitting at the bottom of a dark pit, it's hard to believe in daylight. That's why the Bible speaks so clearly on the fleeting nature of human feelings and the eternal nature of God's presence and His love. He sends you dawn after night, spring after winter, joy after sorrow, to remind you that even in the depths of sorrow, there is the height—and the light— of His love.

> The LORD hath heard the voice
> of my weeping. The LORD hath heard
> my supplication; the LORD will
> receive my prayer.
>
> PSALM 6:8–9 KJV

God has not abandoned you in your weeping. Neither does He judge you for your feelings, nor does He offer you a useless platitude in response to your sorrow. Instead, He comforts you by opening His arms to you, inviting you to talk to Him about your feelings and the depth of your emotions. Even more, He promises He will listen. Go to Him in confidence, even if you're not sure what to say. He is listening to you.

Sharleen, isn't it comforting
that the Father sees our tears!
Your great comforter[71]!!

Emptiness

It was not with perishable things such as silver or gold that you were redeemed from the empty way of life handed down to you from your forefathers, but with the precious blood of Christ, a lamb without blemish or defect.

1 PETER 1:18–19

A deep feeling of emptiness drives many to addiction, despair, and risky behavior. Without a sense of meaning and purpose in their lives, who could blame them? Maybe you find yourself in that very place—empty through and through—but you don't have to live that way. God loves you and He has a purpose and plan for your life—a plan that will challenge you and bring you joy and fulfillment. Let Him fill you with His Holy Spirit and show you who you were created to be.

I pray that you, being rooted and
established in love, may have power,
together with all the saints, to grasp
how wide and long and high and
deep is the love of Christ, and to know
this love that surpasses knowledge—
that you may be filled to the measure
of all the fullness of God.

EPHESIANS 3:17–19

Empty calories lurk in foods of no nutritional
value. Similarly, empty emotions are hidden in
foolish thoughts, selfish pursuits, and meaning-
less activities. They leave you unfulfilled, never
satisfying your real needs. God's love isn't like
that—it's deep, refreshing, renewing, restoring,
and loaded with spiritual nutrients. Breathe it
in! Swallow it! Fill yourself with it! You will
never feel empty again.

Endurance

Let us run with endurance
the race that is set before us,
looking unto Jesus, the author
and finisher of our faith.

HEBREWS 12:1–2 NKJV

You long to scream "enough!" and turn
your back on everything, but you don't. At
times like this, God raises your spiritual
eyes to Jesus, the one who not only walks
with you but has gone before you to the end.
Trust Him to take you to the finish. There
you will thank Him for making it possible
for you to endure present hardship and reap
the eternal reward of achieving His
purpose for your life.

When your endurance is fully
developed, you will be perfect and
complete, needing nothing.

JAMES 1:4 NLT

How easy it would be to give up! And the
truth is, many people would. Yet deep in
your heart you know God asks you to carry
on until you receive God-given release.
Why? Because He has full spiritual maturity
in mind for you. You may be unable to figure
out how your current situation can lead you
to a fuller, more joyful tomorrow, but God
knows. Put your trust in Him as you
continue on the way He has laid out for you.

Envy

Love is patient, love is kind.
It does not envy, it does not boast,
it is not proud.

1 CORINTHIANS 13:4

When envy fills the heart, there's no room left for love. If you have been sidetracked by envy, ask God to help you regain your thoughts and emotions by forgiving you and putting you back on the right path. Once the Lord sweeps your heart clean, you will have a dwelling place fit for humility, kindliness, compassion, and love.

> Don't for a minute envy careless rebels; soak yourself in the Fear-of-God—That's where your future lies. Then you won't be left with an armload of nothing.
>
> —Proverbs 23:17 MSG

You see people living in carefree disregard of God's "thou shalt nots." When they appear so lighthearted and happy, it's hard to not envy them. But you should not. Their lives are headed nowhere. Turn your admiring glance instead to God's Word and read His promises for those who walk rightly. There is great comfort in knowing that following Him will bring you a lifetime—and eternity—of joy.

Eternal Life

[Jesus said,] "I tell you the truth,
whoever hears my word and believes
him who sent me has eternal life
and will not be condemned; he has
crossed over from death to life."

JOHN 5:24

When you're tempted to live for the moment, consider this: God has given you eternal life right now. God means for you to give up a human, shortsighted perspective and live as if you're living for eternity—because you are. Ask God to allow His Spirit to stretch your spiritual sight beyond this moment. Let Him show you what matters for all eternity; then commit yourself to live in it.

[Jesus said,] "God so loved the world that he gave his one and only Son, that whoever believes in him shall not perish but have eternal life."

JOHN 3:16

"Why would almighty God love me?" you ask. "And why would He open heaven to me when I've done nothing to deserve it?" Yes, God's unconditional love is beyond human understanding, but it's there for you. His plan of salvation is all about taking who you are and making you who you were created to be. No matter how strongly you may feel you don't deserve God, embrace Him as firmly and as tenderly as He embraces you.

Example

To this you were called,
because Christ suffered for you,
leaving you an example, that you
should follow in his steps.

1 PETER 2:21

Even Jesus' closest disciples—men and women who traveled with Him during His earthly ministry—did not always follow His example. At times they bickered among themselves, doubted His words, misunderstood His ministry, and denied they even knew Him. Nonetheless, Jesus' healing forgiveness was there for them, just as it is for you. Ask Him and He will teach you how to walk in His footsteps.

Be an example to the believers
in word, in conduct, in love,
in spirit, in faith, in purity.

1 TIMOTHY 4:12 NKJV

When you consider how many people you influence every day through your words, attitude, and actions, you realize how often you set a less-than-stellar example. God uses these times to impress on you how much He wants you to make Him a vital part of your life—not just when it's easy but every day, every hour, every minute. Let your entire life become an example of His love for you.

Expectation

In the morning, O LORD, you hear my
voice; in the morning I lay my requests
before you and wait in expectation.

PSALM 5:3

You have taken your heartfelt requests to
God, and now you are waiting for His
response. Don't grow impatient. Instead,
relish this time of hopeful expectation.
Rehearse the ways God has come through for
you in the past. Allow thanksgiving to flow
freely from your lips. Like a child on the day
before her birthday, enjoy a confident excite-
ment concerning what God is going to do on
your behalf. He is a gracious Father who
can be trusted without hesitation.

> My soul, wait silently for God alone,
> for my expectation is from Him.
>
> PSALM 62:5 NKJV

Sometimes people fail to live up to your expectations, and sometimes you fail to live up to the values and standards you have for yourself. As you take your hurt, your embarrassment, your shame to God, don't forget His unchangeable love for you. He has promised you the gift of His Holy Spirit to give you strength and comfort, and you should expect no less. He will never fail you.

Experience

We know that in all things God works for the good of those who love him, who have been called according to his purpose.

ROMANS 8:28

Perhaps God is permitting you to undergo an unhappy or hurtful experience, and you understandably wonder why. How can He stand by and let you suffer? While the reason why may remain unanswered this side of heaven, His care for you and involvement in your life is a given. He will use this experience to draw you closer to Him, and in it He will bring about good.

> You will show me the way
> of life, granting me the joy of
> your presence and the pleasures
> of living with you forever.
>
> PSALM 16:11 NLT

How long has it been since you allowed
yourself to experience the spiritual joys
of life? Don't let the day's troubles, a busy
schedule, and other distractions strip you
of the everyday pleasures God has set before
you. Consider the fact He has called you
to be His own. Meditate on His presence
in your life and what it means to you. Give
thanks today for the blessings of the day,
and experience His love for you!

Failure

If we are unfaithful, he remains
faithful, for he cannot deny who he is.

2 TIMOTHY 2:13 NLT

You have fallen down, and now what? God is waiting to pick you up again, to dust you off, to comfort and strengthen you so you can go on. Even if you've fallen because you strayed from God's commandments, His strong arms still wait for you. All you need do is call out to Him and ask Him to help you get back on your feet again. God is waiting. Reach up to Him!

Everyone born of God overcomes the world. This is the victory that has overcome the world, even our faith.

1 JOHN 5:4

You are living your faith, but to some people you're a failure. You fail to measure success by the world's standards, and you fail to go along with popular thinking and adopt ungodly values as your own. Let your soul be glad when people call you a failure, because it proves your faith is evident to others. In God's eyes, you have conquered the world. You have rich fellowship with Him and a future brighter than the sun.

Family Life

Bear with each other and forgive whatever grievances you may have against
one another. Forgive as the Lord
forgave you. And over all these virtues
put on love, which binds them all
together in perfect unity.

COLOSSIANS 3:13–14

No family is perfect, and nearly everyone will at
some time hurt, betray, and disappoint a family
member. In extreme cases it may be necessary to
distance yourself. But in all cases, it is necessary
to forgive. Let God judge the person or people who
caused the pain. To you He says, "Forgive." When
you do, you will no longer harm yourself with the
corrosive emotions of anger and resentment.
Instead, you will become more like Christ,
who long ago forgave you.

Live in harmony
with one another.

ROMANS 12:16

Why all the arguments, the bitterness, the
ugly words? In your home, everyone feels
tense and defensive, and you know this is
not what God intends for your family. Let
Him put things right, beginning with you.
Ask His Spirit to show you how to live in
godly harmony with all the members of your
family. Let Him teach you the words and
actions that create genuine affection and
lasting unity. Let God's peace begin with you
and comfort everyone with His presence.

Faults

Confess your faults one to another,
and pray one for another,
that ye may be healed.

JAMES 5:16 KJV

Criticism hurts. While your first reaction is, quite naturally, to retaliate, God has an alternative in mind. Listen to the words of your critic, He says. If your critic has pinpointed a fault in your conduct or character, give thanks you have someone in your life who is frank and truthful enough to tell you where you need to make changes. Ask the Holy Spirit to help you mature and grow in this area.

All Scripture is inspired by God
and is useful for teaching,
for showing people what is wrong
in their lives, for correcting faults,
and for teaching how to live right.

2 TIMOTHY 3:16 NCV

If you feel uncomfortable when you read God's commandments and hear His guidelines for your life, good! The discomfort you feel when facing your faults means the Holy Spirit is at work in you, molding you more and more into a living, breathing, active, vibrant follower of Jesus Christ. Welcome your discomfort. Pray about the faults God's Word points out, and learn what you need to do to overcome them.

Fear

I will fear no evil, for you are with
me; your rod and your staff,
they comfort me.

PSALM 23:4

Do you find yourself trembling when
television newscasters predict hard times
ahead? Could things really get as bad as they
say? Take heart! God reaches out to you, as
He has to His people throughout history,
and offers His comfort in a world full of
uncomfortable news and troublesome
events. No matter what happens or doesn't
happen, your all-powerful and all-knowing
God is your strength and salvation. You can
rest at ease in Him.

> "Fear not, for I have redeemed you; I have summoned you by name; you are mine."
>
> ISAIAH 43:1

In a world of more than six billion souls, fear of becoming "just a number" ranks high among modern-day stressors. God removes the reason for your nagging fear of anonymity when He says to you, "I know your name" and "You are mine." He loves you personally, and He claims you personally. In Jesus Christ, you possess an eternal identity as a forgiven and beloved child of God.

Forgiveness

You are a forgiving God, gracious
and compassionate, slow to anger
and abounding in love.

NEHEMIAH 9:17

Perhaps the sin was huge, and you're still
suffering its consequences. Even though you
feel deeply sorry for what you did and have
apologized to those you hurt, guilt burdens
your heart and weighs your spirit. Do not
let that sin continue on its damaging rampage
through your soul. Instead, give your sorrow
to the God who is bigger than any sin you
could possibly commit. Be comforted by His
promise of restoration and renewal,
and go forward in forgiveness.

Make allowance for each other's faults, and forgive anyone who offends you. Remember, the Lord forgave you, so you must forgive others.

COLOSSIANS 3:13 NLT

No one wants to be the first to say "I'm sorry." No one jumps to take responsibility for a misspoken word, a hurtful act, a mismanaged situation. But without someone possessing the humble courage to extend the hand of peace, no healing can ever take place. Do your part by stepping forward, admitting your part, and asking forgiveness of anyone you may have offended. Jesus forgave you first. True heart healing begins with your willingness to be first in the same way.

Freedom

The LORD sets prisoners free.
PSALM 146:7

We take for granted the ability to move about at will, make independent choices, and manage our own affairs. Many in this world are not so fortunate. They are prisoners. Some are being held in prison for illegal acts; others live in nations where they are prisoners by the will of the government. Still others are prisoners of their own behaviors and excesses. To all the prisoners, God offers the freedom to receive His love and grace, the freedom to know Him and serve Him. Are you in need of freedom?

> Where the Spirit of the
> Lord is, there is freedom.
>
> 2 CORINTHIANS 3:17 NCV

Though some might think of the Christian way as paved with restrictions, just the opposite is true. In the Christian message, God offers you the priceless freedom of living each day free from the chains of guilt, despair, and hopelessness. He has opened to you the door to freedom as His Spirit directs you along the path He has laid out for you—a path leading to genuine happiness and lasting liberty.

Friendship

Wounds from a friend can be trusted.
PROVERBS 27:6

It could be that a friend told you the truth, and it hit you hard. Resentment welled up inside you, and you had to bite your tongue not to say anything. Now you wonder if your friendship will ever be the same again. No, it won't be. It will be better. In her, you have a friend who thinks enough of you to share her deepest concerns, no matter how sensitive or difficult the subject. Give thanks to God for the comfort of a true friend.

As iron sharpens iron,
so a friend sharpens a friend.
PROVERBS 27:17 NLT

The angry words really flew between the two of you, and now you wonder if there's anything left of your friendship. When friendship proves challenging, consider how God can use the situation. He may have something to show the two of you about learning from and growing with each other. He may be pushing both of you toward a deeper, more fulfilling friendship—a friendship meant to last a lifetime.

Fulfillment

A longing fulfilled is a tree of life.
PROVERBS 13:12

Your deepest longings and cherished dreams hold a special place in your heart, and they hold a special place in God's heart, too. He cares what you care about. If you yearn for the fulfillment of your dreams and desires, bring them to the One who knows all about needs, desires, longings, yearnings— and miracles. Trust Him to draw from your dreams the pleasure of godly fulfillment and the satisfaction of true contentment.

> I cry out to God Most High,
> to God, who fulfills
> {his purpose} for me.
>
> PSALM 57:2

You have looked for fulfillment in many places but have discovered nothing but worthless promises. You are not alone! Throughout the Bible, people just like you have raised empty hands to God, begging Him to soothe the deepest longing of their hearts. He heard their pleas, and He hears yours, too. Look to Him. Let His Holy Spirit show you how to find true and lasting fulfillment in living as the beloved child He has created you to be.

Giving

Give freely and spontaneously.
Don't have a stingy heart. The way you
handle matters like this triggers GOD,
your God's, blessing in everything you
do, all your work and ventures.

DEUTERONOMY 15:10 MSG

Fund-raisers and donation campaigns ignite guilt feelings. We begrudgingly pledge a small amount, then we add to our guilt the feeling of being manipulated into giving. God wants a whole new attitude. He stands ready to bless the generous giver, the one who gives with a genuinely cheerful heart. Remember, you possess nothing now that God hasn't given you in the first place. Let your giving flow from a heart of gratitude and love.

[Jesus said,] "Give, and it will be given to you. A good measure, pressed down, shaken together and running over, will be poured into your lap. For with the measure you use, it will be measured to you."

LUKE 6:38

If you want more, give more. That's God's way, and He invites you to make it your way, too. He promises you abundance when you generously share your time, efforts, resources, and abilities. Do so without expecting a reward, knowing all along God will reward you in far greater measure than you can imagine, in far more directions than you expect. Give His way a try, and find out for yourself.

Grace

How rich is God's grace, which he has given to us so fully and freely.

EPHESIANS 1:7–8 NCV

You may be having a difficult time accepting God's undeserved love. Instead, you expect to pay for what you buy and work for what you earn. When it comes to His undeserved love—His grace—you bring the same thinking with you. God's grace, however, works differently. His grace is yours, and it isn't possible to pay for it, earn it, or deserve it. God's grace is yours, not because of you, but because of God.

> From the fullness of his grace
> we have all received one
> blessing after another.
>
> JOHN 1:16

Have you ever shown kindness to someone "just because"? God works in a similar way. He is kind, gracious, and generous toward you "just because." His "just because" relieves you of the burden of striving for His affection and worrying He will fall out of love with you. Today, relax in His grace—His all-embracing love for you— open your arms, and accept His love.

Gratitude

Give thanks to the LORD, for he
is good; his love endures forever.

PSALM 107:1

Do you regularly count your blessings—
the beauty and variety of wildflowers, the
immensity of the evening sky, the power of
the ocean's waves, the majestic heights of a
mountain? Even when you forget to say thank
you, God surrounds you with these things
every day. Name three things in creation
you take pleasure in and give thanks to God
for each of them. Your God made them for
you simply because He wanted you to
enjoy them.

Thank God no matter what happens.

1 THESSALONIANS 5:18 MSG

If you are going through a difficult time in your life, your prayers may sound more like a list of woes than a song of thanksgiving. God wants you to bring to Him your cries of pain, but He also invites you to offer Him your thanks for the good things happening in your life. This is how He reminds you that you and the situation you're facing remain in His hands. Be thankful, because God is present with you—loving and comforting you—every moment of every day.

Sharleen, you shared with me
how grateful you feel because
of spending hours with your
mom. What wonderful memor

Honesty

Good people will be
guided by honesty.
PROVERBS 11:3 NCV

Have you ever been tempted to try a little sleight-of-hand—some deception that will give you an edge over someone else or a privilege you want? Even if we pride ourselves on being clever, God calls it something else: dishonest. For all who strive to follow Him, God sets clear directions to guide thought, speech, conduct, and relationships. With the help of the Holy Spirit, commit yourself to honesty in all you say and do.

> Light shines on those
> who do right; joy belongs to
> those who are honest.
>
> PSALM 97:11 NCV

When you're honest and forthright in all things, you never need worry about covering your tracks or being exposed. You can live with a lightness of spirit unknown to those who must glance over their shoulders in fear of being found out. Ask God to show you where you need to act in a more upright and blameless way. With the help of His Spirit working in you, resolve that your relationships and dealings will be marked by godly honesty.

Hope

We who have fled to take hold of the
hope offered to us may be greatly
encouraged. We have this hope as an
anchor for the soul, firm and secure.

HEBREWS 6:18–19

Dear Sharleen,

I'm sure it comforting that your mom

W ithout hope, you may feel as if you're *put*

being swept along by chaotic currents, unable *her*

to grasp anything solid. God wants you to know *HOPE*

that He is about to reach you, lift you up, and *in Jesus!*

set your feet on the firm ground of His Word

and His promises. Though He might not reveal

to you the reasons behind current circum-

stances, He invites you to place your hope in

Him, holding firmly and securely to the

certainty of His love and care for you.

> No one whose hope is in you will
> ever be put to shame.
>
> PSALM 25:3

God has given us His promises in order to provide sure footing in a tumultuous world. He knew we wouldn't be helped by promises filled with ambiguity and double-talk, so He gives it to us straight. Put your hope in Me, He says, and you won't be disappointed. No one will call you a fool—not after they see your God working on your behalf. Placing your hope in Him is a no-risk proposition, because He will never fail you.

What a promise!!

Humility

With humility comes wisdom.
PROVERBS 11:2 NLT

In a misguided desire to appear humble,
some people intentionally downplay their
abilities and achievements. Your abilities
and achievements, however, are unique gifts
your God has given to you. Godly humility
would have you accept them with pure gratitude and do your best to use them to their
fullest. When someone praises you, thank
your thoughtful friend then add, "To God be
the glory!" This is heavenly humility—and
the height of wisdom.

Humility and the fear of
the LORD bring wealth
and honor and life.

PROVERBS 22:4

Though no one seems eager to pick up a
person fallen from the pedestal of pride,
God is willing. If you find you have to pick
yourself up after a humiliating feat of your
own making, know this: God still loves you.
He desires to hold you close and help you
learn from your experience. Even at your
lowest point, you are precious to Him. Give
Him your hand and He will help you find
your footing again.

Illness

"I am the LORD who heals you."

EXODUS 15:26 NKJV

Have you thought of your illness as a mirror for God's power? When you remain faithful to Him despite your weakness, refusing to give in to despair, people notice. They wonder, "Where does she get her courage?" "How can he remain so optimistic?" Ask the Holy Spirit to reveal His presence in you and use your weakness to reflect His strength. In your illness, people will see the power of God, healer of body and soul.

> Heal me, O LORD, and I shall
> be healed; save me, and I shall be
> saved: for thou art my praise.
>
> JEREMIAH 17:14 KJV

In sickness and in health," the traditional wedding vow declares, and God declares the same to you. Your sickness may diminish your ability to enjoy life right now, but it cannot diminish God's presence in your life or affect His control over all aspects of your well-being. Pray for His healing then wait on Him, confident in His solemn, unbreakable vow to remain with you "in sickness and in health" forever.

Indecision

Preserve sound judgment and discernment, do not let them out of your sight; they will be life for you, an ornament to grace your neck.

PROVERBS 3:21-22

You don't want to make the wrong decision, so you weigh the pros and cons in your mind over and over, spending sleepless nights wondering what to do. Now would be a good time to stop tossing and turning and put the matter in God's hands. Only He knows the outcome of all possible scenarios. Study His Word on the topic, bring to Him your best thinking on the matter, and open yourself to the guidance of His Spirit. Then make your decision with certainty and confidence.

> I will praise the LORD,
> who counsels me; even at night
> my heart instructs me.
>
> PSALM 16:7

When you're faced with a decision, you have a wise counselor in God's Word. Open the Bible, because in it God has revealed His will and His guidelines for the lives of His people, a necessary foundation for any good decision. You also have a wise counselor in His Holy Spirit. Let Him teach you how to pray about the decision you need to make. When you do these things, you will discover His answer.

Intolerance

What does the LORD require of you?
To act justly and to love mercy and
to walk humbly with your God.

MICAH 6:8

When you find yourself easily irritated by others, God wants you to look within yourself. Take stock of your feelings and make an honest assessment of your attitude. With the help of the Holy Spirit, turn away from intolerance. Let His Spirit work in you a heart of compassion, a heart willing to forgive, to accept differences, and to walk humbly with your God.

He who despises his neighbor sins,
but blessed is he who is
kind to the needy.

PROVERBS 14:21

Even in the most conscientious heart, intolerance finds a place to fester. It can raise its ugly head with one disapproving thought of "those people." Invite the Holy Spirit into your heart to banish any feelings of intolerance you may harbor. Ask Him to open your spiritual eyes so you will see God's presence in others, finding Him reflected in their eyes as He is reflected in yours. Then think of "those people" accordingly—as children of God created in His image.

Laughter

[God] will yet fill your mouth
with laughter and your lips
with shouts of joy.

JOB 8:21

The old saying might ring true for you right now: "Laugh and the world laughs with you; weep and you weep alone." Yet you know you're not alone when you weep. God remains at your side with the comfort of His peace, relief, and, yes, laughter. Seem impossible? Not with God. Not when you immerse yourself in His presence today and bathe in the certainty of a better tomorrow. Let Him fill your life with laughter!

> My. . . sisters,
> be full of joy in the Lord.
>
> PHILIPPIANS 3:1 NCV

If you have placed your hope and faith in God, you have every reason to be happy. You know who you are and whose you are. You have set your heart on doing His will, and you hold to His promises to protect and preserve you in any situation you may face in life. Take a moment to thank Him for bringing you into the light of His love, and cultivate a spirit of genuine joy.

Leadership

The greatest among you should be
like the youngest, and the one who
rules like the one who serves.

LUKE 22:26

No matter what your role in life, you're a leader. Either your words and actions lead people toward goodness and virtue, or your conduct turns people away. For this reason, God gives this advice: "Lead by being as happy to walk with the weakest as with the strongest. Lead by being as happy to serve others in an unnoticed, unsung capacity as to take center stage." Follow the example of Christ, who comforted even His enemies.

> Follow my example,
> as I follow the example of Christ.
>
> 1 CORINTHIANS 11:1

If you want to learn about leadership, look at the life of Jesus Christ. Though the Son of God, He did not use His status to intimidate others or amass power, but to serve both the powerful and the weak. This is the example Jesus has set for you. Never shirk your responsibility to those beneath you in authority, education, or social status. Instead, do everything you can to bless the lives of others.

Loneliness

A father to the fatherless, a defender
of widows, is God in his holy dwelling.
God sets the lonely in families.

PSALM 68:5–6

No one has come to take the place of the one
no longer in your life, and you're not sure
anyone really could. You ache with loneliness.
These days are tough, and they're not days
God wants to prolong. He sends people—
relatives, friends, even strangers sometimes—
to lift loneliness from you and bring you into
the company and companionship of others.
Ask Him to open your eyes and heart to those
He sends to comfort you.

[God said,]"Never will I leave you; never will I forsake you."

HEBREWS 13:5

You know what it's like to feel lonely in a crowd, because you feel that way right now. Even though many people surround you, you realize not one of them truly understands what you're going through. But do you believe God understands you—truly understands? He does, you know. And He yearns for you to let Him fill your loneliness with His presence and the fullness of His compassion and care.

Loss

I consider everything a loss
compared to the surpassing greatness
of knowing Christ Jesus my Lord.

PHILIPPIANS 3:8

You've lost something or someone that meant the world to you, and now all you can see is a big hole where your future used to be. If you let God step into that big hole, you'll see Him fill it up, spill out, and tower over it. Where emptiness scared you moments before, abundance invites you now. God asks you to come with Him while He walks you safely through your sorrow and makes of it a renewed tomorrow and a new future.

"Whoever finds his life will lose it,
and whoever loses his life
for my sake will find it."

MATTHEW 10:39

Perhaps you have never told anyone how many of your dreams and desires you have given up for the sake of doing God's will. When it comes to sacrifice, few answer His call, but you did. He knows, and because you have suffered the calculated loss of your own plans and agenda, you will find your gains to be more than you could have imagined possible.

The loss of your mom is great but He is there to fill it.

Marriage

This is the message you
heard from the beginning:
We should love one another.

1 JOHN 3:11

Every marriage has its rocky patches, but it's possible that in yours a few rocky patches have begun to merge into a road of gutted potholes. Have you and your spouse prayed about your marriage? Ask the Holy Spirit to come into your lives, and let Him show you where the love lies among all those stones. Allow God, the God of love, who created marriage to be a blessing to the two of you, smooth the path ahead. He is willing and able to help.

> Understand this, my dear brothers
> and sisters: You must all be quick
> to listen, slow to speak, and slow
> to get angry. Human anger does not
> produce the righteousness God desires.
>
> JAMES 1:19–20 NLT

Time has eroded mutual respect, and habit has taken away the simple courtesies and small surprises that once made your relationship special. This is not what you want for your marriage; it's not what God wants, either. Invite Him to help both of you commit yourselves to needed changes in how you treat each other. Begin with your own heart, where the God of love waits to comfort, renew, restore, and bless your married life.

Ministry

He has made us competent as
ministers of a new covenant—not of
the letter but of the Spirit; for the
letter kills, but the Spirit gives life.

2 CORINTHIANS 3:6

Caring for and comforting others is a profound privilege. With God's Spirit at work in you, let your everyday words and actions comfort and bless others just as God has comforted and blessed you. Your ministry makes you a love-sharer rather than a lawgiver. Maybe you feel you have nothing to share with others, but you do. God loves you, and knowing that enables you to love others.

"When you give a banquet, invite the poor, the crippled, the lame, the blind, and you will be blessed. Although they cannot repay you, you will be repaid at the resurrection of the righteous."

LUKE 14:13–14

Complaints and criticisms hurt, and you might just as soon serve only those people who know how to say thank you. Rest assured God hears you. He knows what it's like to shower people with blessings only to have them congratulate themselves for their good fortune. Yet He continues to bless, and He invites you to follow Him in His ministry. You will hear His comforting thank-you, because He knows.

Mistakes

Happy is the person whose sins are
forgiven, whose wrongs are pardoned.

PSALM 32:1 NCV

Admitting guilt isn't easy for anyone. It's
uncomfortable and embarrassing. But when
we take full responsibility for our sins, God
can bring us comfort and confidence. You,
too, have made mistakes; we all have. The
good news is that we aren't doomed by the
mistakes we've made—not at all. With God
there is room for pardon. Tell Him about
your mistakes, and let Him help you find a
new beginning.

[Jesus said,] "Forgive us our sins, as we have forgiven those who sin against us."

MATTHEW 6:12 NLT

The weaknesses, mistakes, and sins of others affect your life, sometimes bringing serious and lasting harm to you and those you love. You have a right to feel angry, but God offers a better alternative. He urges you to forgive, because forgiveness is the only way to prevent bitterness from taking root in your soul. Compare the "right" of bitterness and the privilege of forgiveness. Choose to forgive.

Money

My God will meet all your
needs according to his glorious
riches in Christ Jesus.

PHILIPPIANS 4:19

God knows how you feel when money runs
out at the end of the month. He has compassion on you in your concern for those dependent on your ability to meet their needs.
Let Him remind you of something: He's in
the need-meeting business, too. The God
who long ago met your most pressing spiritual need does not abandon you in this, your
earthly need. Take all your needs to Him in
prayer, for He hears and answers.

> Keep your lives free from the
> love of money and be content
> with what you have.

HEBREWS 13:5

God doesn't ask you to live without money, but He warns you against the love of money. He wants to free you from the spiritually corrosive sins of greed and envy, and He wants to release you from the bondage of a never-ending list of must-haves. Turn from a love of money and the things it can buy. Ask His Spirit in you to become your most cherished possession, and you will find a rich contentment in everything.

Motives

Serve him with wholehearted devotion
and with a willing mind, for the LORD
searches every heart and understands
every motive behind the thoughts.

1 CHRONICLES 28:9

We claim publicly we're asking for no reward but seek acclaim privately when no reward comes our way. If you find yourself harboring offense, check the motives behind your charitable acts. God already has. Ask Him to replace selfish motives with selfless ones and to instill in you a spirit of compassion, kindness, and generosity. On the outside, you'll continue doing the good things you've been doing. On the inside, you'll be doing them for the right reason.

> Pursue righteousness, faith, love
> and peace, along with those who
> call on the Lord out of a pure heart.
>
> 2 TIMOTHY 2:22

Though your motives are pure toward others, you will encounter those whose hearts aren't pure, and it hurts to find out someone has used you for their own purposes. When that happens—and it almost certainly will at one time or another—take comfort in God. You can be sure that even when others are untrue, God never wavers. He is always thinking of you, putting your best interests first.

Obedience

The proof that we love God comes
when we keep his commandments and
they are not at all troublesome.

1 JOHN 5:3 MSG

If you have broken one of God's commandments and now see the reason why He put
that commandment there in the first place,
you've learned an important lesson. Why
repeat it? He has given you His commandments not to burden you with outdated rules
and undue regulations but for your physi-
cal, emotional, and spiritual well-being.
Embrace all His commandments and obey
them, and you will live in the full
freedom He intends for you.

If anyone obeys his word, God's love
is truly made complete in him. This
is how we know we are in him.

1 JOHN 2:5

If a camera were to record your every word
and action today, what would those watch-
ing the film learn about you? Would they be
able to see that you love God, that you belong
to Him? God is pure and holy, and when we
strive to live by the commandments He's
given us with sincere and humble hearts,
others see the resemblance. They can tell
that we are His children.

Obstacles

God will strengthen you with his own great power so that you will not give up when troubles come, but you will be patient.

COLOSSIANS 1:11 NCV

Perhaps you are facing a mountain in your life—a circumstance so tall and fierce that you have given up before you even started. You're sure there is no way around it, no solution, no hope for you. Take comfort in the fact that you are not facing your mountain alone. God is with you. While your strength is small, God's is great. He may lead you around, over, or help you carve a path right through the middle. Take His hand and somehow you will overcome.

> He will not let you be defeated.
> He who guards you never sleeps.
>
> PSALM 121:3 NCV

Discrimination. Ridicule. Mockery. The obstacles towering in front of you look insurmountable. From your vantage point, if you were to stray just a little from God's way, you could get around the problem and minimize its effect on your life. But consider God's vantage point. He has traveled this way before you, and He knows there are no safe detours. Trust Him to lead you to the other side the right way—His way.

Offenses

I have swept away your offenses like a cloud, your sins like the morning mist.

ISAIAH 44:22

If you have ever watched the morning sun burn away the fog, recall the image when you come before God in prayer. Any offense against God you have ever committed—either intentionally or unintentionally—has been burned away in the light of His forgiveness. Offenses no longer cover you, and guilt no longer shrouds your heart. God has done this for you because He loves you. Respond in joyous thanksgiving today!

Love makes up for all offenses.
PROVERBS 10:12 NLT

False love denies offenses and lives an illusion, but real love acknowledges the offense—and covers it with a compassionate, forgiving heart. Blind love says "nothing happened" and hides in the shadows, but real love says "I forgive you" and begins a new day. What kind of love do you show toward others? Pray for real love, the kind of love God has first shown you. Real love covers. Real love forgives. Real love lasts for eternity.

Past

This is what God says. . .
"Forget about what's happened;
don't keep going over old history."

ISAIAH 43:16,18 MSG

A parent, a child, a spouse just can't forget—and won't let you forget, either. Or maybe it's the other way around. In either case, the past is poisoning the present. Invite God into the picture and ask Him to help you apply His antidote to this cycle of unhealthy and hurtful arguments and accusations. His antidote? Repentance. Forgiveness. Commitment to put the past behind you. God's comfort thrives even in the midst of conflict.

> Forgetting the past and straining
> toward what is ahead, I keep
> trying to reach the goal and get
> the prize for which God called me
> through Christ to the life above.
>
> PHILIPPIANS 3:13–14 NCV

Your past continues to haunt you. Why wouldn't it? What you did and who you were back then leave nothing but shameful memories. God was there, too, and He saw everything. He is here now, however, and He sees an older, wiser, and completely forgiven child of God. His forgiveness gives you the go-ahead to continue with your life, renewed and energized, with your focus on Him and a new eternity.

Patience

Patience is better than strength.
PROVERBS 16:32 NCV

I'm not a patient person!" You've heard it said, and perhaps you've even said it yourself. Unfortunately, the statement supports a false idea about patience. Rather than an inborn personality trait given only to some, patience is a gift of the Holy Spirit worked in the hearts of those who love Him. Godly patience allows you to respond to life's trying situations with serenity and self-control, sure evidence of your continuing walk with God.

> Let us not become weary in doing
> good, for at the proper time we will
> reap a harvest if we do not give up.
>
> GALATIANS 6:9

Things aren't happening quickly enough, and you're feeling frustrated. Pause for a moment and compare your timetable with God's timetable. Evidently they don't match! Instead of fighting against His gracious will, put your trust in it. Let Him unfold the hours, days, and years to you in His own time. His time is, without fail, the right time. Learn from Him the difference godly patience can work in your heart, mind, and spirit.

Peace

You, Lord, give true peace to
those who depend on you,
because they trust you.

Isaiah 26:3 NCV

Daily stress, nagging worries, and ceaseless
squabbles make you long for a place—an hour—
of peace. You don't need to look for a serene
spot, however, and you don't need to arrange a
special time to rest your heart in God's peace.
He has it for you right now, right where you
are. Give God all those things that drive out
peace—name them, hand them over, and don't
grab them back again! Then take comfort in
the peace He has for you.

> A heart at peace gives
> life to the body.
>
> PROVERBS 14:30

Without question, mind and body are linked. God made us that way! His gift of spiritual peace not only soothes a troubled mind by replacing worry with trust, fear with faith, but it also permits a tired, nervous body to get a good night's sleep. Let God fight the battles taking place in your mind, and let your heart rest in His peace. Commit yourself to Him, the healer and restorer of life.

Perfection

All have sinned and fall short of the
glory of God, and are justified freely
by his grace through the redemption
that came by Christ Jesus.

ROMANS 3:23–24

You may have spent years trying to reach
perfection, but perfection remains out of
your grasp. Your futile striving has landed
you right where God wants you—in His arms,
admitting your utter lack of power to make
yourself perfect. Now you're ready to hear
what He has done for you. Long ago, He de-
clared you perfect by sending Jesus Christ to
remove your imperfections. Only He has
the power to do so, and He did.

> To all perfection I see a limit;
> but your commands are boundless.
>
> PSALM 119:96

You may look with awe at the perfection of the stars on a dark, clear night, and melt in joy at the sight of a newborn's perfect eyes, ears, fingers, and toes. With the same sense of wonder, consider God's commandments, spoken by God for your daily guidance and eternal good. He sets His commandments before you this day, inviting you to meditate on the boundless perfection of His words and take them, in their entirety, into your heart.

Persecution

Who shall separate us from the love
of Christ? Shall trouble or hardship or
persecution or famine or nakedness or
danger or sword? . . . . No, in all these
things we are more than conquerors
through him who loved us.

ROMANS 8:35, 37

As the Holy Spirit immerses your soul in the
sweetness of God's love, your attitude and behavior undergo noticeable changes. Now you're
more discerning in your choices and more
thoughtful about what you say and do. Some
people, however, will clamor for the "old you"
back, even resorting to name-calling and slander when you refuse. Don't let their persecution
sway you, but call on God, whose strength and
comfort are yours in all situations you face.

> Everyone who wants to live
> a godly life in Christ Jesus
> will be persecuted.
>
> 2 TIMOTHY 3:12

You know how it is when someone is successful; many times people will applaud them publicly while saying and doing hurtful things behind their backs. When you begin to live a life of peace and joy as God's child, there will be those who will smile to your face but secretly resent you for it. When that happens, you must forgive. Use those situations as opportunities to let others know that they can have what you have. All they have to do is ask.

Perspective

"My thoughts are not your thoughts,
neither are your ways my ways,"
declares the LORD. "As the heavens
are higher than the earth, so are my
ways higher than your ways and my
thoughts than your thoughts."

ISAIAH 55:8–9

We plan, God laughs." While the saying gets a chuckle, we're usually not chuckling when our plans go awry. But step back and look at the situation from another perspective—God's perspective. He sees your future as clearly as He sees your past and present, and He knows how to get you from here to there. Ask the Holy Spirit to help you look from God's perspective—and laugh with the joy of knowing you remain under His watchful care!

Do not be shaped by this world; instead be changed within by a new way of thinking. Then you will be able to decide what God wants for you; you will know what is good and pleasing to him and what is perfect.

ROMANS 12:2 NCV

When you live for the moment, your perspective focuses on what will bring you instant pleasure and immediate gratification. The Holy Spirit has opened to you a deeper, longer, and broader perspective—an eternal perspective. Now you're disposed to put aside selfish desires in favor of godly choices, and you're willing to weigh the spiritual consequences of your actions. Practice seeing with an eternal perspective every day, and prepare to notice eternal results.

Pleasing God

Our only goal is to please God.
2 CORINTHIANS 5:9 NCV

When you have a specific goal in mind, you take every opportunity and use every resource available to you to reach your goal. The goal of living a God-pleasing life is no different. Look for opportunities in your day to do those things you know God wants you to do. Use the resources you have on hand right now to strengthen your faith, increase your understanding of His Word, and serve others with Christlike love in your heart.

Beloved, if our heart condemn us
not, then have we confidence
toward God. And whatsoever we
ask, we receive of him, because
we keep his commandments, and do
those things that are pleasing in his sight.

1 JOHN 3:21–22 KJV

If you have been waiting to get your life in
order before you focus on pleasing God,
God has a happy surprise for you. God has put
your life in order through the earthly ministry
of Jesus. As His forgiven child, respond in
genuine joy and gratitude by living to please
Him. Worship Him, obey His commandments, and show compassion on others. By
focusing on pleasing God, you will find your
life in God-pleasing order.

Potential

I have filled [you] with the Spirit
of God, with skill, ability and
knowledge in all kinds of crafts.

EXODUS 31:3

Have you reached your full potential? If you're still breathing, you haven't! God has blessed you with a wide range of talents for you to tap throughout your life. Enrich every stage of your life by following your interests, broadening your knowledge, and developing your abilities. You will be surprised at the variety of God-given gifts you possess—and experience the sheer enjoyment of embracing your potential.

> In [God] you have been enriched
> in every way—in all your speaking
> and in all your knowledge.
>
> 1 Corinthians 1:5

Ask God to show you where you are not using the potential your faith has given you. Consider the things you already know about God and His commandments, and use your knowledge to introduce others to God's love. List your abilities—you have more than you think!—and consciously use them to serve others. Use your Spirit-given potential to walk as an effective, exciting, and powerful woman of God.

Prayer

"You will call upon me and come and
pray to me, and I will listen to you.
You will seek me and find me when
you seek me with all your heart."

JEREMIAH 29:12–13

*It is awesome
how God wants conversation with you!*

You may have heard many differing opin-
ions on the subject of prayer. What God says
about prayer, however, is simple. When you
pray—whether kneeling, sitting, or standing;
whether in time-tested words or in your own
words—He hears you. He responds in a way
designed to increase your faith and develop
a strong relationship with Him. Continue
to pray and pray faithfully, because through
prayer, God offers you the comfort of daily
conversation between your heart and His.

The LORD hath heard
the voice of my weeping. The
LORD hath heard my supplication;
the LORD will receive my prayer.

PSALM 6:8–9 KJV

When you don't receive what you've
prayed for, it's easy to conclude God is telling you no. Not so! He has promised to hear
your prayers, but are you listening for His
answer? If He chooses to not give you exactly
what you have prayed for, He has chosen
something better for you. If He chooses to
remain silent today, He is encouraging you
to continue praying, placing your trust in
Him and His wisdom.

Priorities

Fear God and obey his commands,
for this is everyone's duty.

ECCLESIASTES 12:13 NLT

Knowing God gives you a new perspective on your work, family life, and friendships. You see these God-given blessings for what they are, and you want to tend to them mindfully and well. Like a broad umbrella, however, God stands over and above you and all He has given you. Never let anything in your life take priority over God, who shelters you with His continuing guidance, comfort, and care.

> Seek his will in all you do, and he
> will show you which path to take.
>
> PROVERBS 3:6 NLT

Financial troubles, medical issues, relationship problems, and similar difficulties tend to occupy first place in thoughts, time, and energy. Yet this is exactly the time your priorities need to be in order! If you allow a crisis to dominate, anxiety continues to consume you, and you lose sight of the help, strength, and solace you have in God. Whether things are going smoothly or not so smoothly, make sure God stays first in your life.

Protection

I've run to you for dear life.
I'm hiding out under your wings
until the hurricane blows over.

PSALM 57:1 MSG

When bad things happen, we tend to wonder, Isn't God supposed to protect us from disaster? Rest assured your God knows and cares about what is taking place in your life, and His arms of comfort and consolation are there to enfold you in His love. All the while, His Holy Spirit is working in you to guard and keep your soul from anything that would threaten your eternal salvation. Hold firmly to God, and discover your immediate solace and your ultimate safety in Him.

> The eternal God is your refuge,
> and underneath are the everlasting arms.
>
> DEUTERONOMY 33:27

God's commandments always work to protect your soul and very often your mind, emotions, and body from danger. He sets His guidelines under you to keep you away from anything capable of stealing the good in your life and covering you with guilt, pain, and regret. Pray for a deeper appreciation of the refuge He has set for you in His commandments and will for your life.

Provision

[God] gives food to those
who fear him; he always
remembers his covenant.

PSALM 111:5 NLT

We serve a God of miracles, and sometimes
miracles come in the simplest provisions—
food enough for the next meal, a warm coat
for your child, a place to sleep at night. When
the checkbook gets low and the bills are
stacking up, He is there to point you to help,
to see that you and yours have the basic needs
of daily living. Thank Him for both the small
miracles and the great ones.

God will generously provide all
you need. Then you will always have
everything you need and plenty left
over to share with others.

2 CORINTHIANS 9:8 NLT

In a culture replete with consumer goods,
the line between needs and wants tends to
blur not only in ads and commercials, but in
our thoughts as well. God's mind, however,
is clear on the subject of needs and wants—
He knows the difference. Trust Him to give
you those things He knows you need, and
give thanks to Him for all He provides.
If you think about it, you'll realize He
has given you plenty to share with
others, too!

Purpose

We are God's workmanship,
created in Christ Jesus to do good
works, which God prepared
in advance for us to do.

EPHESIANS 2:10

Some people say life is merely a meaning-
less accident of nature. Perhaps the idea
has entered your mind and thoughts, too.
If so, you understand why God in His Word
declares repeatedly the value He places on
human life. He created you out of His eternal
love, and He has made you who you are and
placed you where you are for His divine purpose. Open your heart and spirit to take hold
of the great purpose God has for your life.

> We constantly pray for you,
> that our God may count you
> worthy of his calling, and that by
> his power he may fulfill every good
> purpose of yours and every act
> prompted by your faith.
>
> 2 THESSALONIANS 1:11

If you could plan the course of your children's lives, would you doom them to failure and despair? Of course not. You love your children. Your plans for them would be all good. Your heavenly Father feels the same about you. And He does have the power to set in place a plan and purpose for your life. You can be certain that His will includes only the best for you—the best of joy, of love, of peace, of abundance, of success.

Questions

On the day I called,
You answered me; You made me
bold with strength in my soul.

PSALM 138:3 NASB

What is this?" "Where are we now?" "How come this is this way?" One thing children know how to do is ask questions. Mothers know, however, that their children might not be ready or able to hear the answers to all their questions, so they answer the ones they can and tuck the others away. Your heavenly Father hears your questions, all of them. But He doesn't give you all the answers at once. Trust Him to know what you can handle. Answer in faith.

170

> "Call to me and I will answer you
> and tell you great and unsearchable
> things you do not know."
>
> JEREMIAH 33:3

If you have ever worked with children, you know they will sometimes ask a question but not listen to your answer. As God's child, avoid doing the same thing. Pose your questions to God, and then listen to His answer. You may not like what you hear—it may be difficult to accept or sound unreasonable to you. Ask the Holy Spirit to deepen your understanding and give you the power to accept even the most difficult of God's unsearchable answers.

Respect

A kindhearted woman gains respect.
PROVERBS 11:16

When you consistently show kindness and caring for others, sincerely honoring their humanity, their work, and their rights, you gain their respect. They cannot help but notice the respect you offer to everyone, from the lowliest person to the highest, from the youngest to the oldest, from the weakest to the most powerful. Ask the Holy Spirit to help you show heartfelt respect to others, because this is the way you gain respect in return.

Make it your ambition to lead a
quiet life, to mind your own business
and to work with your hands, just as
we told you, so that your daily life may
win the respect of outsiders and so that
you will not be dependent on anybody.

1 THESSALONIANS 4:11–12

Who you are in public and in private
shapes your character and the perception
people have about you. Do you consistently
act in a way deserving of others' respect?
Do your words and actions put others in
the best light? Ask the Holy Spirit to show
you what you could change to heighten the
respect others have for you and to build
respect for the presence of God in your life.

Responsibility

To do what is right and just is more acceptable to the LORD than sacrifice.

PROVERBS 21:3

Whether or not God ever calls you to make a huge personal sacrifice for Him, He definitely calls you to take on the responsibilities He has placed in front of you. These responsibilities may not differ in essence from anyone else's responsibilities, but your willing and uncomplaining acceptance of them marks you as His child. Perform them to the best of your ability, and in all you do, do the right thing.

Pay careful attention to your own
work, for then you will get the
satisfaction of a job well done, and
you won't need to compare yourself
to anyone else. For we are each
responsible for our own conduct.

GALATIANS 6:4–5 NLT

God has loaded you with more responsibilities than you can handle—or so you think!
In fact, He never gives you responsibilities
without also giving you the strength to manage
your tasks well. When you feel overwhelmed,
don't focus on getting out from under your
responsibilities. Instead ask the Holy Spirit
to build you up in faith and attentiveness
so you can carry your own load with
dignity and a true appreciation of your
God-given abilities.

Rest

[Jesus said]: "Are you tired?
Worn out? Burned out on religion?
Come to me. Get away with me and
you'll recover your life. I'll show
you how to take a real rest."

MATTHEW 11:28 MSG

You know how it is. Busy schedules and pressure to perform crowd in on every side. But God never intended for you to be spent and weary in body and soul. Not only does He permit us to rest; He insists on it. Ask God to show you where you can open up some time to rest your body and nourish your soul, close your eyes, and relax in His comforting arms.

> Rest in the LORD, and wait
> patiently for Him.
> PSALM 37:7 NKJV

You need more than rest for your body.
Your mind and emotions also need to be
renewed. God understands how difficult
it is to step away when so many people are
depending on you. Ask Him to help you find
respites in the storms of life, special times,
however brief, when you can rest your body
and soul. Listen as He says, "Come, My
weary daughter, and I will give you rest."

Restoration

"I will restore you to health and heal your wounds," declares the LORD.

JEREMIAH 30:17

Have you prayed many times for God's restoring hand in your life, and yet you can't seem to get over those memories and emotions that cause you so much pain? God's healing sometimes happens overnight, but most often it takes time. Take comfort in knowing that each day in some small way, He is bringing you through, giving you strength, creating for you a future based on His love.

> The God of all grace, who called
> you to his eternal glory in Christ,
> after you have suffered a little while,
> will himself restore you and make
> you strong, firm and steadfast.
>
> 1 Peter 5:10

No matter how low your sufferings may have brought you, God works to lift you up and build you up. He is a God who takes no pleasure in seeing you broken in body or in spirit, but He takes great pleasure in restoring you and filling you with more of His spiritual gifts of patience, faith, and strength of character. Lift your eyes to God's unchangeable promise to heal you, and keep your trust in Him.

Reward

[Jesus said,] "Blessed are you when people insult you, persecute you and falsely say all kinds of evil against you because of me. Rejoice and be glad, because great is your reward in heaven."

MATTHEW 5:11–12

Though it seems noble to say, "I'm not doing this for a reward," Jesus promises a sure and certain reward to those who follow Him in obedience. His promise works to comfort you when your commitment to Him makes you the object of insult, ridicule, or slander. Don't let these things take away your peace, but instead be glad. Let insults remind you: Great is your reward in heaven.

You know that the Lord
will reward everyone for
whatever good he does.

EPHESIANS 6:8

Through the ministry of Jesus Christ, God
has done for you what you could never do
for yourself—secure your salvation. He has
satisfied your greatest need. Now His Holy
Spirit working in you prompts you to do the
things He invites His followers to do. That is,
show compassion, give practical assistance
to those in need, and share your spiritual
wisdom and understanding. He even offers
you an incentive—eternal reward from your
Lord and God.

Service

There are different kinds
of service, but the same Lord.

1 CORINTHIANS 12:5

Even after you commit yourself to following God's will, jealousy can creep into your
heart. You notice her work gets so much
more recognition than yours and her gifts
seem so much greater. God would have you
turn from the temptation to compare your
work with anyone else's. Both of you in your
different roles serve the same God. Put
your confidence in Him as you serve Him
and others in every way open to you.

[Jesus said,] "Whoever serves me must follow me; and where I am, my servant also will be. My Father will honor the one who serves me."

JOHN 12:26

Following Jesus requires you to serve others wherever you are. Never for a moment wait for other circumstances, a more convenient time, a later date! The moment you commit yourself to following Jesus Christ, you give yourself to serving others by showing compassion and kindness, by offering help and counsel, by bringing His love wherever you are right now. Pray for His Spirit to open your eyes to see opportunities to serve Him.

Spiritual Struggle

Put on the full armor of God so that you can take your stand against the devil's schemes. For our struggle is not against flesh and blood, but against the rulers, against the authorities, against the powers of this dark world and against the spiritual forces of evil in the heavenly realms.

EPHESIANS 6:11–12

You cannot fight temptation on your own. Deadly spiritual forces work to pull you away from God and into the grip of sin, turmoil, and despair. Pray for a realistic awareness of the forces fighting against you, and let the Holy Spirit equip you for the struggle. Fill your mind and heart with His Word, dedicate yourself to listening only to the still, small voice of God inside you, and rely on His power and strength.

> Pursue righteousness, godliness,
> faith, love, endurance and gentleness.
> Fight the good fight of the faith.
>
> I TIMOTHY 6:11–12

Through your faith, God's Spirit has put into your heart the vision of His will for your life. It's like a precious gift inside you, building you up and giving you the desire and motivation you need to fight for your spiritual life. Keep doing the right thing, continue learning, and persist in praying that your faith will grow and strengthen in the struggle. Spiritual warfare is happening because you've moved away from the grip of wickedness and into the arms of God. Give thanks!

Starting Over

This is what the LORD says—your
Redeemer, the Holy One of Israel. . .
"I am about to do something new.
See, I have already begun!
Do you not see it?"

ISAIAH 43:14, 19 NLT

When the Holy Spirit brought you to faith in
Jesus Christ, your life started over. You may
or may not have realized it at the time, and
since then you might have slid right back into
doing things the same old way and thinking the same old thoughts. Your new life in
Christ, however, is not a onetime event. It
happens each time you come to Him and ask
for renewal and refreshment. Seek Him,
and start over again today.

Create in me a pure heart,
God, and make my spirit right again.

PSALM 51:10 NCV

The psalmist had strayed so far from God's
will for his life that he dropped to his knees
and prayed for a whole new heart and spirit.
If you have strayed, you can join the psalmist
in his plea. Ask God to give you a clean heart,
a restored spirit, and a chance to walk with
Him again. Trust in Him to forgive you, and
you will see the miracle of a brand-new life.

Strength

I can do everything through him
who gives me strength.

PHILIPPIANS 4:13

Has a new opportunity opened for you?
Maybe after thinking and praying about it,
you feel drawn to take on the project, but a
nagging doubt holds you back. Are you strong
enough? If you keep looking at your own
strength, you will pass on the opportunity.
If instead you look to God and realize it's
His strength He's offering, you can take on
the challenge with confidence. In Him you
have great strength!

The Lord is faithful,
and he will strengthen and
protect you from the evil one.

2 THESSALONIANS 3:3

God never expects you to hold on to your faith by your own strength. He knows the weakness of all human hearts, and He knows all about the temptations you deal with every day. With His own strength, God will defend you! Ask the Holy Spirit to give you His strength and power, so you will exercise your spiritual muscles and move beyond your frailty. Where you are weak, God is strong.

Suffering

I consider that our present sufferings
are not worth comparing with the
glory that will be revealed in us.

ROMANS 8:18

When you suffer, it's hard to think of anything except your suffering, and that's why
God provides something else to think about,
something to balance the pain you are feeling now. Despite the circumstances of your
suffering, open your spiritual eyes to how
He is using the situation to reveal to you and
others His presence and His power. To break
through the darkness of suffering, take your
hope and comfort from the shining light of
His unfailing love.

> Those who suffer as God
> wants should trust their souls
> to the faithful Creator.
>
> 1 Peter 4:19 NCV

It's possible that through no fault of your
own, you are enduring the pain of grief, despair, and hopelessness. God understands
the depth of your suffering, even your anger
that life should treat you so unfairly. Allow
His Spirit to use your suffering as a starting
point for His healing as He restores hope
and instills His strength in you. Entrust
yourself to your faithful God, for in Him
you have life, peace, and comfort.

Surrender

[Jesus said,] "If you try to hang on to
your life , you will lose it. But if you give
up your life for my sake and for the sake
of the Good News, you will save it."

MARK 8:35 NLT

You may have thought about the concept of
surrendering yourself to God, but you've hes-
itated because you want to be who you are—
not a puppet of someone else. Don't worry!
After all, God is the one who created you to be
the unique woman you are. He has no intention of tampering with that. His goal is just to
offer stability in your emotions and thought
life and to enhance your talents and abilities.
Surrender to the hand of God means fulfillment of your deepest God-given desires.

> Give yourselves completely to God.
> Stand against the devil, and the devil
> will run from you. Come near to God,
> and God will come near to you.

JAMES 4:7–8 NCV

Sometimes when we aren't entirely convinced we want to go all out for God, we try to keep Him at a safe distance. Yet to go all out for Him is what God is asking each of us to do. He knows how hesitance keeps us vulnerable to the pull of doubt, the fear of life, and the pain of reverting to our old ways. Let Him close the distance between you. You will be amazed by how comforting it can be to be fully surrendered to Him.

Temptation

Because [Jesus] himself suffered when
he was tempted, he is able to help
those who are being tempted.

HEBREWS 2:18

Jesus has passed this way ahead of you. In
His humanity, He was tempted and He knows
firsthand its power and pull. He has compassion on the weakness of human flesh, and
He is not ashamed to travel with you in your
struggle. He wants you to live free, without
the tentacles and restrictions of destructive
behaviors and unhealthy desires. The challenge is great, but He has promised to walk
with you, comforting and strengthening you
every step of the way.

No test or temptation that comes your way is beyond the course of what others have had to face. All you need to remember is that God will never let you down; he'll never let you be pushed past your limit; he'll always be there to help you come through it.

1 CORINTHIANS 10:13 MSG

Your faith and commitment to God will be tested, and often tests come in the form of deeply personal, private, even foul temptation. Don't be fooled into thinking you're the only one ever tempted in this way. You're not! Take the temptation to God in prayer, asking Him to lift its burden from you. No matter how long you may struggle against it, you have the God-given strength to resist it. And because God is there to help you, you will never walk alone.

Time

There is a right time and
a right way for everything.

ECCLESIASTES 8:6 NCV

Pure and simple, time is a gift. Each
second, minute, hour, and day is yours to
use as you please. *Not so fast,* you might be
thinking. *All my time is filled with work and
responsibilities and taking care of other
people.* That's true, your time might be
dictated by other choices you have made, but
it is still yours. Ask God to help you squeeze
in some time for yourself. He'll show you
where to find it.

> [God] has made everything
> beautiful in its time. He has also
> set eternity in the hearts of men;
> yet they cannot fathom what God
> has done from beginning to end.

ECCLESIASTES 3:11

You wonder, sometimes with great anxiety, what time will bring. Let God put your mind at ease. Remember, He was present at the beginning and will be present at the end. He knows everything that has happened or will happen in between, including all the days and years of your life. Entrust the time you've been given to God, and do not fear for the future. His hand is on eternity.

Trials

When you have many kinds of troubles,
you should be full of joy, because you
know that these troubles test your faith,
and this will give you patience. Let your
patience show itself perfectly in what you
do. Then you will be perfect and complete
and will have everything you need.

James 1:2–4 ncv

God never discounts the pain you go through
during life's difficult trials, but He always
finds a way to use your pain for your advantage.
Through trials, He reveals to you the quality of
your faith, so you can see where your weaknesses are and take these things to Him in
prayer. Without trials, you might never realize
the deep comfort of His presence or the
penetrating glow of His eternal love.

God blesses those who patiently
endure testing and temptation.
Afterward they will receive the crown
of life that God has promised
to those who love him.

JAMES 1:12 NLT

God permits trials to pit your faith against
life's harsh realities. It is the only venue
in which you are able to see His power and
appreciate His unwavering commitment to
you. You might know that God loves you, but
the reality comes in the difficult times. You
might acknowledge that He is wise, but you
won't appreciate it fully until you have
seen Him guide you to safer ground.
Rejoice in your trials, for they help
you learn who God is in your life.

Trust

Trust the LORD with all your heart,
and don't depend on your
own understanding.

PROVERBS 3:5 NCV

You might have been taught to depend on yourself, and perhaps others admire you as a confident and self-determined woman. Eventually, however, you will reach the limits of your understanding, and that's where you will find either frustration—or God. Use fully the gifts of intellect and ability He has given you, but at the same time, put your heart's trust in God. He alone knows no limits.

> Those who know the LORD
> trust him, because he will not
> leave those who come to him.
>
> PSALM 9:10 NCV

You've learned. You're more cautious than
you used to be about putting your trust
in anyone or in any thing. But remember
where you had put your broken trust—in
the faithfulness of a person; in the loyalty
of your employer; in the strength of the
economy. All these earthly things can fail
you. React not by withholding trust but by
putting your ultimate trust in God. Then all
other aspects of trust will, in turn, fall into
the right places.

Wisdom

Wisdom is a tree of life to those
who embrace her; happy are
those who hold her tightly.

PROVERBS 3:18 NLT

Perhaps you thought you had a great idea,
but it turned out to be a big mistake. You
wish you had listened to warnings and given
the matter more thought. Let God use this
teachable moment to give you the gift of
wisdom. The wisdom from above may seem
counterintuitive at times, but you can be
certain it won't fail you. It is embedded in
the timeless nature of God, who sees from
eternity to eternity.

If any of you needs wisdom,
you should ask God for it. He is
generous to everyone and will give
you wisdom without criticizing you.

JAMES 1:5 NCV

Wisdom seems like such a lofty goal, yet it's what God offers to you freely and generously simply for the asking. You see, His wisdom has nothing to do with graduate degrees but everything to do with a humble willingness to sit in the school of the Holy Spirit. Open His Word and learn from it. Meditate on its meaning and apply it to your heart and your life. This is genuine wisdom.

Work

"Do not work for food that spoils, but for food that endures to eternal life, which the Son of Man will give you. On him God the Father has placed his seal of approval."

JOHN 6:27

All of us must work for the food that sustains our lives here on earth. But God would remind us that we should work for our spiritual food as well. The Bible says that Jesus is the Bread of Life. Your relationship with Him provides you with food for your spirit, food like wisdom, understanding, insight, and counsel—food like joy, peace, love, and patience. Work hard to provide your spirit with all the spiritual food it needs.

> Serve wholeheartedly, as if you were
> serving the Lord, not men, because
> you know that the Lord will reward
> everyone for whatever good he does,
> whether he is slave or free.
>
> EPHESIANS 6:7–8

Sometimes you may find your work unsatisfying, perhaps because you feel unappreciated or unenthusiastic about your daily responsibilities. While praying about any changes you might want to make, remind yourself of the reality of all godly work: God is the boss. Talk to Him about your work in light of the fact that, in all you do, you are doing it for Him. There's great comfort in seeing all you do as your gift to Him.

Worry

[Jesus said]: "Don't worry. . . .
Your heavenly Father already
knows all your needs."

MATTHEW 6:31–32 NLT

Worry will steal your life if you let it. And
yet it is nothing more than the anticipation of
trouble that most likely will never come your
way. It has no substance and no power except
in your mind. God asks you to replace your
worry with a firm trust in His love and concern
for you. He knows all that is in your future, all
of your needs, and He is committed to caring
for you. Surrender your mind to God and don't
give worry a second thought.

[Jesus said,] "Give your entire attention to what God is doing right now, and don't get worked up about what may or may not happen tomorrow."

MATTHEW 6:34 MSG

God considers worry a negative commodity in your life because it takes the place of trust in His willingness and ability to take care of you. When worry visits your heart, banish it by reminding yourself how completely God has taken care of you in the past. List the blessings in your life today that shout of His protection and love. Then entrust the future to this same God. See for yourself you have nothing to worry about.

Scripture Index

Proverbs

Ecclesiastes

Isaiah

Notes

Notes

Notes

Notes

Notes

Notes